STUDENT WORKBOOK

Dr. John L. Feirer

Keyed to the 1994 edition of
BEGINNING WOODWORK

GLENCOE
McGraw-Hill

New York, New York
Columbus, Ohio
Mission Hills, California
Peoria, Illinois

Glencoe/McGraw-Hill

A Division of The **McGraw·Hill** *Companies*

Send all inquires to:
Glencoe/McGraw-Hill
3008 W. Willow Knolls Drive
Peoria, IL 61614-1083

ISBN 0-02-677602-2

Printed in the United States of America
4 5 6 7 8 9 10 11 12 VER 01 00 99 98 97

TABLE OF CONTENTS

TO THE TEACHER

This student workbook is designed for use with the textbook *Beginning Woodwork*. It is planned as a teaching aid for the teacher and as a workbook for the student in completing the work in a first woodworking course.

All of the questions in the student workbook are objective, for ease of completion, checking, and correction. The workbook is planned so that the chapters can be used by students individually or in group activity.

Students can be asked to complete the chapters in one of several different ways:

1. Each student may progress at his or her own rate of speed and complete the sheets as fast as possible.

2. The teacher may assign a lesson in the textbook as homework and then use the workbook for objective testing the next day.

3. Students may spend some time in supervised study covering the related information of the course.

4. Students can be assigned sections of the book for outside study and at the same time may be asked to complete the student workbook chapters.

Other material has been included that will simplify the teaching and be of value in:

1. Organizing the class.
2. Keeping records of cost of materials.
3. Having an accurate safety record.
4. Keeping the results of student planning together.

There is also space on page 6 for additional regulations. Thus all the written material for the course in woodworking can be kept in one place in a well-organized fashion.

HOW TO USE THIS STUDENT WORKBOOK

This workbook includes study chapters and all other material you need for keeping a record of your progress in woodworking.

Complete the following:

1. Fill in the *Student Information Sheet* (page 6). This will help your teacher become better acquainted with you.

2. Make a list of the regulations that you are expected to follow.

3. Read the *Safety Pledge* (page 11) carefully. Sign it after you have agreed to obey the regulations.

4. Fill in the *Cost of Materials* chart (pages 7 and 8). These costs will be used when making the bill of materials for each project.

5. Keep a record of your assignments in the student personnel and cleanup organization of your class (page 9).

6. Make a plan for each product you build. There is a sample plan sheet on page 10.

7. Complete each study chapter. The textbook pages you should study are given on the first page of each study chapter. Place the answers to the questions in the blank spaces along the left edge of each page. Each answer is worth one point. (Example: If one question contains two different answers, each one is worth one point. If a question calls for an answer that consists of more than one word, that answer is still worth one point.) At the upper right of each chapter heading is a place for you to write your score. Also shown there is the total number of points in the chapter. You can keep a record of all your study chapter scores on page 12.

There are several different kinds of questions in each chapter. Samples of the types of questions used are shown below. Study the examples so that you will know the correct way to answer each question.

1. True-False (T or F): Read the statement carefully and decide whether it is true or false. If the statement is true, put a T in the answer blank to the left of the question. If the statement is false, put an F.

SAMPLE: _____*T*_____ Washington, D.C., is the capital of the United States. (T or F)

2. Multiple Choice: Read the question and the possible answers. Write the letter of the correct answer in the answer blank to the left of the question.

SAMPLE: _____ *C* _____   A state that is east of the Mississippi River is *(one right)*
  a. Arkansas.
  b Missouri.
  c. Illinois.
  d Iowa.

3. Completion: Study the sentence and decide what word or words would correctly complete the thought. Write the word or words in the answer space to the left of the question. Do not write your answer in the blank in the question itself.

SAMPLE: _*Jupiter*_____   The largest planet in the solar system is _____.

SAMPLE: _*bee*_____   Milk is to a cow as honey is to a _____.

SAMPLE: _*red*_____   The primary colors are _____, _____, and _____.
  _*yellow*_____
  _*blue*_____

4. Identification: In the answer space to the left of the question, write the correct name of the item or items pictured.

SAMPLE: Name the common eating utensils shown in Fig. A.

a. _*knife*_____

b. _*spoon*_____

c. _*fork*_____

Fig. A

5. Matching: Match each item in the left-hand column to an item in the right-hand column. Write the letter of the correct choice in the answer blank to the left of the question. Sometimes you will be asked to match an item to the lettered section of a picture.

SAMPLE: Match the sports items to the games for which they are used.

_*a*_____	1. goal posts	a. football
_*d*_____	2. hoop	b. tennis
_*c*_____	3. puck	c. hockey
_*b*_____	4. racquet	d. basketball

SAMPLE: Match the names of common eating utensils to the appropriate picture in Fig. A.

_*b*_____	1. spoon
_*a*_____	2. knife
_*c*_____	3. fork

6. Logical Order: Study the series of sentences. Decide how they should be arranged for correct step-by-step order. Place the number of the step after the corresponding letter in the blank on the left.

SAMPLE: Place the following steps in the order in which you would complete them to effectively study a chapter of *Beginning Woodwork.*

_*1*_____	a. Read the chapter title and anticipate what the chapter is about.
_*3*_____	b. Read the chapter in its entirety.
_*2*_____	c. Scan the major headings.
_*4*_____	d. Answer the questions in the appropriate study chapter of this guide.

STUDENT INFORMATION SHEET

Please print:
1. Name _____
               LAST   FIRST   MIDDLE

2. Home address _____

3. Home phone number _____

4. Year in school _____

5. School last attended _____

6. Parents' names:

   Father _____

   Mother _____

7. Parents' occupations:

   Father employed by _____

   Mother employed by _____

8. Hobbies or outside interests _____

   _____

9. Previous shop experience _____

   _____

10. Name of family doctor _____

    Address _____

    Doctor's telephone number _____

SAFETY AND REGULATIONS

1. _____

2. _____

3. _____

4. _____

5. _____

6. _____

7. _____

8. _____

9. _____

10. _____

11. _____

12. _____

COST OF MATERIALS

Lumber

KIND	COST PER BOARD FOOT	KIND	COST PER BOARD FOOT
Mahogany			
Walnut			
Maple			
Oak			
Birch			

Panel Stock:

KIND	GRADE	THICKNESS	COST PER SQ. FOOT
Plywood			
Hardboard			
Particle board			

COST OF MATERIALS (cont'd.)

Screws, Nails and Other Items

NO. OR SIZE	KIND	COST PER _____
	Screws	
	Nails	
	Dowel	
	Sandpaper	
	Hardware	

Finishing Materials:

KIND	COST PER _____

PERSONNEL AND CLEANUP ASSIGNMENTS

Date   **Job**

From _____ to _____   _____

From _____ to _____   _____

From _____ to _____   _____

From _____ to _____   _____

From _____ to _____   _____

ACCIDENT REPORT

1. Name of Injured _____

   Address _____

   Telephone _____

   Home Room _____

2. Nature of injury (Cut, scratch, foreign matter in eye, etc.)

   _____

3. Tools or machines involved _____

4. Witnesses to the accident: Name _____

   Address _____

   Name _____

   Address _____

5. Treatment: First aid _____ By Whom _____

   Physician _____ Address _____

   Hospital _____ Address _____

6. Cause of Accident (Poor condition, wrong procedure, etc.) _____

   _____

   _____

7. Correction (What will be done to prevent future accidents) _____

   _____

   _____

   Your Name _____

PLAN SHEET

Name _____ Grade _____

_____

NAME OF THE PRODUCT   DATE STARTED   DATE COMPLETED

Bill of Materials:

NO.	SIZE			NAME OF PART	MATERIAL	UNIT COST	TOTAL COST
	T	W	L				

Tools and Machines:

_____

_____

_____

_____

_____

_____

_____

_____

_____

_____

_____

_____

_____

_____

Procedure or Steps:

1. _____

2. _____

3. _____

4. _____

5. _____

6. _____

7. _____

8. _____

9. _____

10. _____

11. _____

12. _____

13. _____

14. _____

15. _____

RECORD IN THE WOODSHOP

Class Tests

No. 1 _____

No. 2 _____

No. 3 _____

No. 4 _____

No. 5 _____

No. 6 _____

No. 7 _____

No. 8 _____

Product Grades

1 _____
    Product   Grade

2 _____
    Product   Grade

3 _____
    Product   Grade

4 _____
    Product   Grade

5 _____
    Product   Grade

6 _____
    Product   Grade

7 _____
    Product   Grade

8 _____
    Product   Grade

SAFETY PLEDGE

I pledge that I will follow all of the safety rules given in the book *Beginning Woodwork* and all of the shop regulations listed on page 6. I will not use a power tool without first getting the permission of the instructor. I will report all accidents to the instructor immediately, no matter how small they are. I will help to maintain a safe shop by tending to my business and by not bothering other students who are busy.

Date _____   Name _____

SCORES

STUDY CHAPTER	POSSIBLE SCORE	NUMBER CORRECT	STUDY CHAPTER	POSSIBLE SCORE	NUMBER CORRECT	STUDY CHAPTER	POSSIBLE SCORE	NUMBER CORRECT
1 & 2	19	_____	26 & 27	17	_____	51 & 52	14	_____
3	21	_____	28–31	23	_____	53 & 54	16	_____
4	15	_____	32	24	_____	55 & 56	14	_____
5	15	_____	33	18	_____			
6 & 7	16	_____	34	20	_____			
8	17	_____	35	19	_____			
9	14	_____	36 & 37	18	_____			
10	10	_____	38	23	_____			
11	18	_____	39	17	_____			
12	26	_____	40 & 41	16	_____			
13, 14, & 15	15	_____	42–45	27	_____			
16, 17, & 18	20	_____	46	14	_____			
19 & 20	16	_____	47	14	_____			
21 & 22	19	_____	48	24	_____			
23	21	_____	49	17	_____			
24 & 25	24	_____	50	17	_____			

Date _____ Name _____

Score (19 possible) _____

Chapters 1 and 2
Exploring Woodworking and Safety
(Text pages 11-27)

_____ 1. The average person in the United States uses only about half as many wood products as the average person in other countries. (T or F)

_____ 2. Woods often used in building construction include *(one wrong)*
   a. pine.
   b. fir.
   c. mahogany.
   d. cedar.

_____ 3. A shop sketch is always needed when you design your own project. (T or F)

4. Arrange in numerical order these steps in making a project. Each answer is worth one point.

_____   a. Plan your work.

_____   b. Read the drawing or make a sketch.

_____   c. Select the materials.

_____   d. Rate the project.

_____   e. Select or design the project.

_____   f. Build the project.

_____ 5. Federal safety standards for the workplace were established by the Safe Work Act. (T or F)

_____ 6. When you are working in the shop, you should roll up your sleeves and tuck in any loose clothing. (T or F)

_____ 7. Goggles or safety glasses are not needed in a beginning woodworking shop. (T or F)

_____ 8. A dull tool is safer than a sharp tool. (T or F)

_____ 9. When carrying sharp tools, always keep the pointed end up and toward you. (T or F)

_____ 10. You should test the sharpness of tools with your finger or hand. (T or F)

_____ 11. Rags used in the wood shop should be kept in a _____ container.

_____ 12. A clean and orderly shop is a safer shop. (T or F)

_____ 13. It is not necessary to get first aid for small cuts or scratches. (T or F)

_____ 14. Every accident in the shop should be reported to the _____.

Chapter 3
Measurement
(Text pages 28-39)

_____   1. The customary (English) system of measurement is used throughout most of the world. (T or F)

_____   2. The modernized metric system is known as the _____ metric system. *(one right)*
   a. IOS
   b. IS
   c. SI
   d. MM

_____   3. The metric base unit for length is the _____.

_____   4. A kilometre is 100 times larger than a metre. (T or F)

_____   5. A millimetre is 1000 times smaller than a metre. (T or F)

Match the seven base units with their symbols.

_____   6. kg   a. metre
                                    b kilogram
_____   7. s   c. second
                                    d. ampere
_____   8. A   e. kelvin
                                    f. candela
_____   9. cd   g. mole
_____   10. m
_____   11. mol
_____   12. K

_____

a. _____   13. A 300-millimetre rule is longer than a 1-foot rule. (T or F)

b. _____   14. Read the measurements shown on the rule in Fig. 3-A.

c. _____

d. _____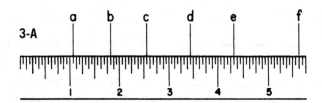

e. _____   3-A

f. _____

_____   15. The total distance around the piece of wood shown in Fig. 3-B is _____.

16. Metric length measurements for woodworking are rounded to the nearest _____.

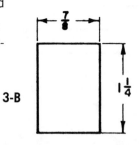

3-B

Chapter 4
Design
(Text pages 40-48)

_____   1. In order to have good design, an object must be _____ and beautiful.

_____   2. Forms like cubes, pyramids, and spheres are made by combining _____.

_____   3. Red, yellow, and orange are examples of warm colors. (T or F)

_____   4. If the height of a picture frame must be 10 inches, then the length should be _____ inches to make the frame in good proportion.

_____   5. The grain of a material gives it its _____.

Match the words in the column on the left with the items in the column on the right.

_____   6. harmony

_____   7. rhythm

_____   8. emphasis

_____   9. proportion

_____   10. balance

a. golden oblong
b. formal or informal
c. repetition of shape
d. parts get along well
e. center of interest

4-A

_____   11. If a project does its job well, it is *(one right)*
a. in proportion.
b. functional.
c. rhythmic.
d. balanced.

_____   12. Figure 4-A shows _____ _____ furniture design.

_____   13. Figure 4-B shows _____ furniture design.

4-B

_____   14. A sanding block is a good example of a _____ project. *(one right)*
a. novelty
b. utility
c. artistic
d. decorative

_____   15. A dining room table is an example of a(n) _____ or decorative project.

Chapter 5
Ordering Materials
(Text pages 49-58)

_____ 1. It is harder to cut with the grain than across it. (T or F)

_____ 2. The broad-leafed tree is classified as a _____.

_____ 3. _____ is a common softwood. *(one right)*
   a. Maple
   b. Oak
   c. Pine
   d. Cherry

_____ 4. Lumber purchased surfaced on two sides is classified as _____.

_____ 5. AD means that the lumber has been _____.

_____ 6. Kiln-dried lumber contains about 6 to _____ percent moisture.

_____ 7. Grade A and Grade B softwood lumber is also referred to as _____ grade.

_____ 8. FAS means _____ _____ _____.

_____ 9. No. 1 and No. 2 hardwoods are better quality than FAS. (T or F)

_____ 10. A board 1″ × 12″ × 12″ is *(one right)*
   a. 2 board feet.
   b. 1 board foot.
   c. 1 square foot.
   d. 1 linear foot.

_____ 11. There are 6 board feet of lumber in a piece of pine 1″ × 6″ × 12′. (T or F)

_____ 12. A piece of stock that is 1″ thick, 12″ wide, and 60″ long contains _____ board feet.

_____ 13. If lumber costs $280.00 per M, it costs _____ cents per board foot.

_____ 14. The most common size of plywood sheet is 4 feet by _____ feet.

_____ 15. Hardboard and particle board are two materials made of wood _____ or fibers.

Chapters 6 and 7
Drawing and Planning
(Text pages 58-68)

_____

1. Most working drawings have _____ views. *(one right)*
   a. three
   b. four
   c. six
   d. one

_____

2. Working drawings most commonly show front, top, and bottom views. (T or F)

a. _____

b. _____

c. _____

d. _____

e. _____

f. _____

3. Name the common lines shown in Fig. 6-A.

a .... d

b .... e

c .... f

6-A

_____

4. The sizes of the parts of a project are shown by the _____.

_____

5. If a project is drawn so that three inches equal one foot, the project is *(one right)*
   a. full-size.
   b. half-size.
   c. one-eighth size.
   d. one-fourth size.

_____

6. In planning your work in the wood shop, you will need a drawing of the project or a shop sketch. (T or F)

_____

7. A rational size is a metric dimension that has been rounded off to a convenient figure. (T or F)

_____

8. A list of all the things you need to build a project is called a _____ of materials.

_____

9. In giving the size of a piece of wood, dimensions should be listed as *(one right)*
   a. width, thickness, length.
   b. thickness, width, length.
   c. length, width, thickness.
   d. length, thickness, width.

_____

10. In making a stock-cutting list, you should add _____ inch to the exact dimension for length.

_____

11. Plywood is cut from a sheet that is $\frac{1}{16}$ inch thicker than the finished thickness. (T or F)

Chapter 8
Using Measuring and Marking Tools
(Text pages 74-82)

_____   1. A 3-foot rule is sometimes called a _____.

_____   2. The _____ rule is used to measure longer stock when exact measurements are not too important.

a. _____   3. Name the tools shown in Fig. 8-A.

b. _____

c. _____

8-A

Match the tools in the left-hand column with their descriptions in the right-hand column.

_____   4. bench rule

_____   5. combination square

_____   6. outside calipers

_____   7. framing square

_____   8. sliding T bevel

a. used to lay out angles other than 45 or 90 degrees
b. used to measure outer diameter of round objects
c. also called a carpenter's square
d. includes a scriber, level, blade, and head
e. comes in 1-, 2-, and 3-foot lengths

_____   9. Marking tools used in woodworking include the *(one wrong)*
    a. lead pencil.
    b. shortblade knife.
    c. pin punch.
    d. scratch awl.

_____   10. Pencil lines should be sanded off. (T or F)

_____   11. In measuring length with a rule, the rule should be held on edge. (T or F)

_____   12. When measuring a board for length, keep the rule parallel with the edge of the board. (T or F)

_____   13. The spur, or pin, of a marking gauge should be sharpened to a wedge shape. (T or F)

_____   14. After the spur, or pin, has been sharpened, you can depend on the scale for accuracy. (T or F)

_____   15. When using a marking gauge, you should always mark across the grain. (T or F)

BEGINNING WOODWORK STUDENT GUIDE

Date _____   Name _____

Score (14 possible) _____

Chapter 9
Making a Layout
(Text pages 83-89)

_____

_____

_____

_____

_____

_____

_____

_____

_____

_____

_____

_____

_____

_____

1. If a dividers is set to a distance of 1⅜ inches, it will draw a circle with a diameter of _____ inches.

2. The circumference of a circle that is 3 inches in diameter is _____ inches.

3. When drawing a circle with the dividers, the dividers should be set to ¼ the diameter of the circle. (T or F)

4. Parts that are exactly the same are called _____ parts.

5. You can divide a board that is 10 inches wide into three equal pieces with a rule by placing the 0 and the _____ inch marks on the edges and drawing marks at 4 and 8 inches. (T or F)

6. A curved line can be divided into equal parts by using the _____.

7. Patterns can be enlarged by using cross-section paper. (T or F)

8. If a pattern in a book is covered with squares that are marked ¼ inch, then to make a full-size pattern, draw squares that are ½ inch in size. (T or F)

9. Another name for a French curve is *(one right)*
   a. regular curve.
   b. irregular curve.
   c. English curve.
   d. drawing curve.

10. A pattern that is identical on both sides is *(one right)*
    a. proportional.
    b. symmetrical.
    c. harmonious.
    d. informal.

11. A pattern that is made of thin wood or metal and used over and over again is called a _____.

12. The radius of the circle in Fig. 9-A is _____ inches.

13. The circumference of the circle in Fig. 9-A is _____ inches.

14. If the original design is on 1-inch squares, you can make it half-size by drawing it on _____ -inch squares.

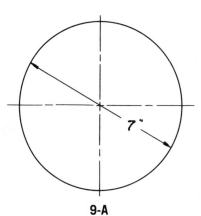

9-A

Chapter 10
Machines in Woodworking
(Text pages 90-92)

_____ 1. Chisels and hammers could be considered machines. (T or F)

_____ 2. Work accomplished over a long distance requires more force than the same work done over a short distance. (T or F)

_____ 3. The resistance caused by the rubbing together of machine parts is called _____.

_____ 4. Machines can increase both force and distance at the same time. (T or F)

_____ 5. All woodworking machines are made up of a combination of _____ simple machines.

_____ 6. All knives, chisels, saws, and axes have _____.

_____ 7. The support point of a lever is called the _____.

_____ 8. The hammer and ax are examples of _____.

_____ 9. A screwdriver and a door handle are examples of the wheel and _____.

_____ 10. A pulley is a wheel that turns around an _____.

Chapter 11
Sawing to a Line with Handsaws
(Text pages 92-99)

a. _____

b. _____

c. _____

d. _____

e. _____

_____

_____

_____

_____

_____

_____

_____

_____

_____

_____

_____

_____

1. Name the parts of the handsaw shown in Fig. 11-A.

11-A

2. The cut made by a saw is called a _____.

3. A crosscut saw for general-purpose cutting should have about eight or nine points per inch. (T or F)

4. The teeth of a ripsaw are knife-shaped. (T or F)

5. Saws should be carried with the heel towards the floor. (T or F)

6. When cutting across grain the saw should be held at an angle of about *(one right)*
   a. 30 degrees.
   b. 45 degrees.
   c. 60 degrees.
   d. 90 degrees.

7. The crosscut saw cuts both on the forward and back strokes. (T or F)

8. As you cut across the grain, keep your eye on the saw, not on the layout line. (T or F)

9. If a saw is moving into or away from the layout line, you should twist the handle slightly to bring it back. (T or F)

10. To prevent a board from breaking off just before the cut is completed *(one right)*
    a. saw faster and beat the break.
    b. hold the end to be cut off as the final short strokes are made.
    c. saw flat across the top.
    d. make several slow cuts.

11. When ripping, the saw should be held at an angle of about *(one right)*
    a. 30 degrees.
    b. 45 degrees.
    c. 60 degrees.
    d. 90 degrees.

12. A handsaw cuts on the forward stroke. (T or F)

13. The steel in a handsaw is hard enough to cut through small nails and screws. (T or F)

14. When cutting plywood to width, use a _____ saw.

Date _____ Name _____

Score (26 possible) _____

Chapter 12
Assembling and Adjusting a Plane
(Text pages 100-105)

_____   1. The largest plane is the _____ plane.

a. _____   2. Identify the parts of the plane shown in Fig. 12-A.

b. _____

c. _____

d. _____

e. _____

f. _____

g. _____

h. _____

i. _____

j. _____

k. _____

12-A

Match the type of plane in the left-hand column with its description in the right-hand column.

_____   3. jack plane

_____   4. smooth plane

_____   5. fore plane

_____   6. jointer plane

a. 18 inches long; used to plane long surfaces and edges
b. 22 inches long; used to plane edges of doors
c. good for general use around the home
d. 14 or 15 inches long; good for rough surfaces

_____   7. For very fine planing, the plane-iron cap should be about _____ inch from the cutting edge.

_____   8. A lever cap screw is tightened or loosened with a screwdriver or the _____ _____.

_____   9. There are two blade adjustments on a hand plane. (T or F)

Match the part to what it does.

_____   10. lever cap

_____   11. throat

_____   12. adjusting nut

_____   13. lateral adjusting lever

_____   14. frog

a. holds plane iron firm
b. opening for shavings to pass
c. provides sidewise adjustment
d. provides support for plane iron
e. turn to raise plane iron

_____   15. A plane should be placed on its side whenever it is not being used at the bench. (T or F)

_____   16. Always plane with the grain to get a smooth surface. (T or F)

Score (15 possible) _____

Chapters 13, 14, and 15
Squaring Operations—Part I
(Text pages 106-114)

_____   1. In squaring up stock, always plane the worst face first. (T or F)

_____   2. A condition in which one side of the board is concave and the other convex is called _____.

_____   3. A board that twists along its length has a defect called _____.

_____   4. Always plane against the grain, never with it. (T or F)

_____   5. Which part (A or B) in Fig. 13-A shows the correct method of applying pressure when planing?

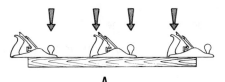 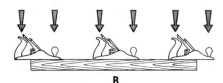

A   13-A   B

_____   6. To remove high spots, the planing should be done at an angle. (T or F)

_____   7. The first, or face, edge must be at _____ angles to the face surface.

_____   8. When planing the first edge, remove as little stock as possible to square it. (T or F)

_____   9. End grain is easier to plane than edge grain. (T or F)

_____   10. The block plane cutter has a chip breaker. (T or F)

_____   11. A block plane cuts end grain well because it is at a high angle and the cutter is set with the bevel down. (T or F)

_____   12. When planing the first end, always select the end that needs the greatest amount of planing. (T or F)

_____   13. When adjusting the plane for end-grain cutting, adjust it to a heavy cut. (T or F)

_____   14. End grain should be planed completely across in one direction. (T or F)

15. One way to avoid splitting off the back edge of stock is to clamp a piece of _____ _____ behind it.

Score (20 possible) _____

Chapters 16, 17, and 18
Squaring Operations—Part II
(Text pages 114-123)

a. _____

b. _____

c. _____

_____

_____

_____

_____

_____

_____

_____

_____

_____

_____

_____

_____

_____

_____

1. Name the parts of the back-saw shown in Fig. 16-A.

2. The backsaw is a fine-tooth ripsaw. (T or F)

3. The backsaw kerf should be made directly on the layout line. (T or F)

4. The surface of plywood must be planed. (T or F)

5. Number in correct order these steps in squaring up stock. Each answer is worth one point.

    a. Plane the second end.

    b. Plane the first, or face, surface.

    c. Plane the first end.

    d. Plane the first, or face, edge.

    e. Plane the second face.

    f. Plane the second edge.

6. When squaring up stock to length, allow about _____ inch for planing.

7. The two kinds of operations done to sharpen tools are grinding and _____.

8. A slow-speed grinder is good because there is little danger of _____ the blade.

9. An oilstone is a fine-grained stone used to _____ cutting edges. *(one right)*
    a. grind
    b. hone
    c. dress
    d. true

10. Mineral oil can be used on an oilstone. (T or F)

11. When grinding a plane iron, the bevel should be about _____ times the thickness of the blade.

12. The correct angle for honing a blade is about _____ degrees.

13. If the cutting edge turns blue during sharpening, it means the edge is overheated. (T or F)

16-A

Date _____

Name _____

Score (16 possible) _____

Chapters 19 and 20
Cutting a Curve, Chamfer, Bevel, or Taper
(Text pages 123-130)

a. _____

b. _____

c. _____

d. _____

_____

_____

_____

1. Name the parts of the coping saw shown in Fig. 19-A.

2. Coping saw blades have teeth similar to a cross-cut saw. (T or F)

3. When using a coping saw with the work held in a vise, the teeth should be pointing away from the handle. (T or F)

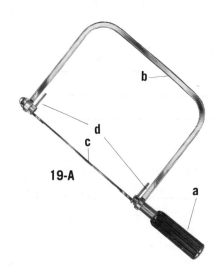

19-A

4. Which saw can *not* be used for sawing curves and irregular shapes?
   a. coping saw
   b. compass saw
   c. backsaw
   d. keyhole saw

Match the terms at the left with their definitions on the right.

_____ 5. chamfer

_____ 6. bevel

_____ 7. taper

a. a slanted surface cut partway down
b. a cut that gradually becomes smaller toward one end
c. a sloping edge or end

_____

_____

8. A chamfer is usually cut at an angle of _____ degrees.

9. A sliding T bevel is used for *(one right)*
   a. checking a 90-degree angle.
   b. laying out and checking odd angles.
   c. checking curved surfaces.
   d. squaring up stock.

_____

_____

_____

10. To set a sliding T bevel to an odd angle, a _____ is used.

11. Use a pencil to lay out lines for a chamfer. (T or F)

12. When planing a chamfer on end grain, make a shearing cut. (T or F)

13. To fit two pieces together to make a V-shape, you must cut *(one right)*
   a. a chamfer.
   b. a taper.
   c. a bevel.
   d. a groove.

Score (19 possible) _____

Chapters 21 and 22
Cutting with Chisels and Gouges
(Text pages 131-139)

a. _____

b. _____

c. _____

d. _____

1. Name the parts of the chisel shown in Fig. 21-A.

21-A

Match the type of chisel on the left with its description on the right.

_____ 2. pointed tang

_____ 3. solid tang

_____ 4. socket

a. has a cup shape at the end of the blade into which the handle fits
b. the blade and tang are one piece
c. the tang extends into the wood handle

_____ 5. A _____ is a short-handled hammer with a large wooden, rawhide, or plastic head.

_____ 6. When removing large amounts of wood, turn the chisel with the bevel side up. (T or F)

_____ 7. A concave surface is one that curves out. (T or F)

_____ 8. In trimming a concave surface, the bevel side of the chisel should be down. (T or F)

_____ 9. In trimming a convex surface, the bevel side of the chisel should be up. (T or F)

_____ 10. A gouge is a _____ with a curved blade.

_____ 11. The size of a gouge is the length of the arc at the cutting edge. (T or F)

_____ 12. The inside-ground gouge is the most common. (T or F)

_____ 13. When beginning to shape a surface with a gouge, always start near the edge of the waste stock. (T or F)

_____ 14. To remove a great amount of waste stock, strike the end of the gouge with a _____.

_____ 15. Whittling should be done with the grain. (T or F)

_____ 16. Only softwoods should be used for whittling. (T or F)

Chapter 23
Other Shaping Tools
(Text pages 140-143)

a. _____

b. _____

c. _____

d. _____

_____

1. Name the parts of the spokeshave shown in Fig. 23-A.

   23-A

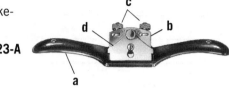

2. The spokeshave is a small cutting tool much like a *(one right)*
   a. chisel.
   b. plane.
   c. saw.
   d. knife.

_____

_____

_____

3. When using a spokeshave, the tool can be pushed or pulled. (T or F)

4. If a spokeshave chatters as it is used, the blade probably isn't exposed enough. (T or F)

5. The spokeshave was first used to shape the spokes of wagon wheels. (T or F)

a. _____

b. _____

c. _____

d. _____

e. _____

_____

_____

_____

6. Name the parts of the file shown in Fig. 23-B.

   23-B

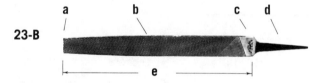

7. The most common files for woodworking are the half-round cabinet files and the _____ wood files.

8. A file is rougher than a wood rasp. (T or F)

9. To clean the teeth of a file or rasp, use a *(one right)*
   a. nylon brush.
   b. cloth.
   c. Surform tool.
   d. file card.

_____

_____

_____

_____

_____

10. A rasp will remove material faster than a file. (T or F)

11. A rasp has individually shaped cutting teeth. (T or F)

12. A multi-tooth (Surform) tool is used like a rasp. (T or F)

13. The teeth of a Surform tool become clogged easily. (T or F)

14. It is safe to use a file or rasp without a handle. (T or F)

Date _____

Name _____

Score (24 possible) _____

Chapters 24 and 25
Drilling and Boring Holes
(Text pages 144-151)

a. _____

b. _____

c. _____

_____

a. _____

b. _____

c. _____

d. _____

_____

a. _____

b. _____

c. _____

d. _____

e. _____

_____

_____

_____

a. _____

b. _____

c. _____

d. _____

e. _____

_____

_____

1. Name the parts of the twist drill shown in Fig. 24-A.

24-A

2. Twist drills up to _____ inch can be used with a hand drill.

3. Name the parts of the hand drill shown in Fig. 24-B.

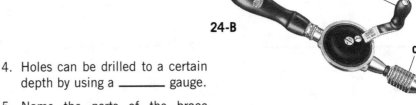

24-B

4. Holes can be drilled to a certain depth by using a _____ gauge.

5. Name the parts of the brace shown in Fig. 25-A.

25-A

6. To bore a hole in close quarters, use a(n) _____ brace.

7. Auger bits most commonly used vary in size from _____ inch to 1 inch.

8. An auger bit that bores a 9/16-inch hole would have No. _____ stamped on the shank.

9. Name the parts of the auger bit shown in Fig. 25-B.

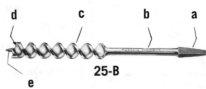

25-B

10. An expansion bit is set to the correct size by adjusting the cutter until the distance from the spur to the feed screw equals the _____ of the hole.

11. The common range of sizes of Foerstner bits is ¼ inch to _____ inches.

Chapters 26 and 27
Making Common Joints—Part I
(Text pages 151-160)

a. _____

b. _____

c. _____

d. _____

e. _____

f. _____

g. _____

h. _____

_____

_____

_____

_____

_____

_____

_____

_____

_____

1. Name the eight basic joints.

2. A joint similar to the edge joint is *(one right)*
   a. a blind dado.
   b. a tongue-and-groove.
   c. a dado.
   d. a mortise-and-tenon.

3. A joint commonly used in making shelves is *(one right)*
   a. a miter joint.
   b. a dado joint.
   c. a lap joint.
   d. a mortise-and-tenon joint.

4. Another name for a blind dado is a _____.

5. The trim around doors and windows is constructed by using a _____ joint.

6. A joint commonly found in better drawer and box construction is *(one right)*
   a. a butt joint.
   b. a dado joint.
   c. a rabbet joint.
   d. a dovetail joint.

7. The common diameters for dowel rod range from _____ to 1 inch.

8. When making a dowel edge joint, the pieces to be joined should be of the same width. (T or F)

9. Dowels should be located every _____ to 18 inches when making a dowel edge joint.

10. The diameter of the dowel should be *(one right)*
    a. one-fourth the thickness of the stock.
    b. one-half the thickness of the stock.
    c. five-eighths the thickness of the stock.
    d. three-fourths the thickness of the stock.

Date _____ Name _____

Score (23 possible) _____

Chapters 28, 29, 30, and 31
Making Common Joints—Part II
(Text pages 160-173)

1. Arrange in numerical order these steps in joinery. Each answer is worth one point.

   _____

   _____

   _____

   _____

   _____

   a. Fitting.

   b. Cutting.

   c. Assembling.

   d. Layout.

2. The best saw for making the shoulder cut for a rabbet joint is a *(one right)*
   a. crosscut saw.
   b. coping saw.
   c. backsaw.
   d. jigsaw.

   _____

3. A dado is a slot cut _____ the grain.

   _____

4. A groove is a slot cut _____ the grain.

   _____

5. A dado joint is a rather weak joint. (T or F)

   _____

6. A router plane is used to cut a miter joint. (T or F)

a. _____

b. _____

c. _____

d. _____

e. _____

7. Name the parts of the router plane shown in Fig. 29-A.

29-A

8. The dado is usually cut to a depth equal to _____ the thickness of the stock.

   _____

9. Lap joints are made by _____ the ends or edges of two boards.

   _____

10. The _____ -lap joint is used to extend the length of material.

   _____

11. To make a T-shaped joint, use a _____ -lap.

   _____

12. The cross-lap joint is made like two extra-wide dadoes. (T or F)

   _____

13. To make a miter joint, the ends of two pieces are cut at equal slants. (T or F)

   _____

14. If a frame has eight sides, the miters are cut at an angle of _____ degrees.

   _____

15. A miter saw is similar to a _____ .

   _____

16. A miter joint is a strong joint. (T or F)

Chapter 32
Clamping and Gluing Up Stock
(Text pages 174-181)

a. _____

b. _____

c. _____

1. Name the clamps shown in Fig. 32-A.

32-A

2. _____ clamps look like large clothespins.

_____

Match the items in the left-hand column with those in the right-hand column.

_____ 3. liquid hide glue

_____ 4. white liquid resin glue

_____ 5. resorcinol glue

_____ 6. powdered resin

_____ 7. powdered casein

_____ 8. flake animal

a. an all-around household glue for mending and furniture making
b. strong, but is not waterproof and cannot be used
   on outdoor furniture
c. best for outdoor furniture and boats
d. good for use on oily woods
e. too much trouble to prepare for small jobs
f. never should be used on oily woods

_____

9. When mixing powdered resin glue, mix _____ parts powder with ½ to 1 part water.

_____

10. _____ glue comes in two separate containers and must be mixed be-fore using.

_____

11. When gluing stock face to face, the stock should first be squared up to rough size. (T or F)

12. Number in correct order these steps in assembling a project. Each an-swer is worth one point.

_____ a. Select the correct kind and number of clamps.

_____ b. Assemble first part of project and clamp.

_____ c. Clamp parts together temporarily.

_____ d. Cut clamp blocks.

_____ e. Decide on how the project is to be assembled.

_____ f. Get all parts together.

_____ g. Mix correct kind and amount of glue.

_____ h. Remove excess glue.

_____ i. Assemble the complete project.

_____ j. Apply the glue.

_____ k. Allow the first section to dry.

Date _____   Name _____

Score (18 possible) _____

Chapter 33
Using Nails
(Text pages 182-188)

a. _____

b. _____

c. _____

d. _____

_____

_____

_____

_____

_____

_____

_____

_____

_____

_____

_____

_____

1. Name the parts of the claw hammer shown in Fig. 33-A.

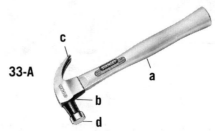

33-A

2. Most nails are made of mild steel or _____.

3. The size of a nail is given by the term "penny" or the letter _____.

4. _____ nails have small heads and are ideal for project making, cabinetwork, and finish carpentry.

5. The length of a 6d nail is _____ inches.

6. A small round-headed brass nail is called an _____ pin.

7. If several nails are installed along the grain line, it may split the wood. (T or F)

8. When nailing in hardwood, it is sometimes a good idea to drill a hole first that is _____ the diameter of the nail.

9. When using a hammer, the handle should be held near the head. (T or F)

10. Bent nails can be straightened and reused by striking them on the side. (T or F)

11. Casing and finishing nails should be driven below the surface of the wood about _____ inch.

12. To drive a nail below the surface, use a _____ _____.

13. One board edge can be fastened to the face or edge of another by _____.

14. Corrugated fasteners hold best when placed at an angle to the _____.

15. When driving a nail into wood, you should keep your eyes on the hammer. (T or F)

Chapter 34
Installing Screws
(Text pages 189-194)

_____

1. Wood screws are made of *(one wrong)*
   a. mild steel.
   b. brass.
   c. aluminum.
   d. cast iron.

_____

2. Screws that are used around the water should be made of _____.

_____

3. Roundhead screws of mild steel are made with a _____ finish.

_____

4. Screw heads may be slotted or _____.

_____

5. Lower gauge size screws are generally used for _____ wood.

a. _____

b. _____

c. _____

6. Name the parts of the screwdriver shown in Fig. 34-A.

34-A

_____

7. A screw-mate drill and countersink is a tool for installing _____ screws.

8. Number in correct order these steps in fastening two pieces of wood with a flathead screw. Each answer is worth one point.

_____

   a. Mark the location of the screw hole in the second piece.

_____

   b. Mark the location of the screw hole in the first piece.

_____

   c. Cut a conical hole with the countersink.

_____

   d. Drive the screw.

_____

   e. Drill the shank hole in the first piece.

_____

   f. Drill a pilot or anchor hole.

_____

9. A No. 5 screw would require a shank hole that is _____ inch in diameter.

_____

10. A pilot hole for a No. 8 screw in softwood would be _____ inch in diameter.

_____

11. The auger bit size to use when plugging a hole for a No. 8 screw would be No. _____.

_____

12. The blade of a plain screwdriver should be slightly smaller than the width of the screwhead. (T or F)

_____

13. After installation, the screwhead can be concealed with a plug or with a filler of _____ _____.

Date _____   Name _____

Score (19 possible) _____

Chapter 35
Installing Hardware
(Text pages 195-198)

_____   1. Cabinet hardware includes (one wrong)
    a. hinges.
    b. handles.
    c. nails.
    d. drawer pulls.

_____   2. Butt hinges can be purchased with either a _____ or solid pin.

_____   3. The recess that is cut in a frame or door for installing a hinge is called a _____.

_____   4. The same number of hinges is needed for doors of all sizes. (T or F)

_____   5. A small door would probably require _____ hinges about 1½ to 2 inches long.

_____   6. Surface hinges are more difficult to install than butt hinges. (T or F)

7. Arrange in numerical order these steps in installing a surface hinge. Each answer is worth one point.

_____   a. Mark location of hinges.

_____   b. Place wedges at the bottom and at one side of the door.

_____   c. Place the door in the opening temporarily.

_____   d. Place the door in the opening and install one screw through each hinge and into the frame.

_____   e. Fasten the hinges to the door itself.

_____   f. Adjust the door until it works correctly.

_____   8. When purchasing door handles and pulls, you also need to buy screws for installing them. (T or F)

                               9. Name three types of common catches.

a. _____

b. _____

c. _____

_____   10. Mending plates are used to strengthen a butt or lap joint. (T or F)

_____   11. The flat corner iron is used to strengthen corners of _____.

_____   12. T plates are used to strengthen the center rail of a _____.

Chapters 36 and 37
Sanding and Preparing Stock for Finishing
(Text pages 198-204)

Match the names of these common abrasives with their descriptions.

_____   1. flint

_____   2. garnet

_____   3. aluminum oxide

a. brown, synthetic abrasive
b. made of quartz
c. reddish brown, hard mineral

_____   4. The coarsest abrasive in the following list is *(one right)*
    a. 400.
    b. 50.
    c. 120.
    d. 30.

_____   5. A good abrasive number for sanding after the project is assembled is 1/0 or No. _____.

_____   6. The surface of sandpaper is covered with sand. (T or F)

_____   7. Always sand across grain, never with it. (T or F)

_____   8. Sandpaper should be used to sand off pencil and knife marks. (T or F)

_____   9. Surfaces that are to be glued should not be sanded. (T or F)

_____   10. A piece of sandpaper wrapped around a dowel rod can be used to sand a _____ curve.

_____   11. Plaster of paris can be used to fill holes and cracks in a wood surface. (T or F)

_____   12. When making a crack filler with powdered resin glue, _____ and water are added to make a thick paste.

_____   13. Oxalic-acid crystals are used in wood finishing for _____.

_____   14. When adding a filler to repair a hole or crack, always add enough filler to make the surface slightly higher than the rest of the wood. (T or F)

_____   15. Scraping is usually done on *(one right)*
    a. open-grained wood.
    b. plywood.
    c. close-grained wood.
    d. hardboard.

16. Number in correct order these steps in preparing wood for finishing.

_____   a. Scrape and/or sand the surface.

_____   b. Repair or fill holes and cracks.

_____   c. Bleach the wood if necessary.

Date _____   Name _____

Score (23 possible) _____

Chapter 38
Wood Finishes
(Text pages 204-207)

Match the proper finish in the left-hand column with the projects in the right-hand column.

_____   1. light mineral oil

_____   2. outside paint or enamel

_____   3. penetrating finish

_____   4. inside paint or enamel

_____   5. standard finish

a. outdoor sports equipment
b. indoor novelties
c. simple outdoor projects
d. furniture and accessories
e. kitchen items

6. Number in correct order the steps in applying a natural finish.

_____   a. Apply a second coat of shellac.

_____   b. Cover the surface with paste wax.

_____   c. Rub down with fine steel wool.

_____   d. Apply a coat of boiled linseed oil.

_____   e. Brush on a coat of white shellac.

7. Number in correct order the steps in applying a standard finish.

_____   a. Seal coat over stain.

_____   b. Seal coat over filler.

_____   c. Stain.

_____   d. Apply filler.

_____   e. Bleach.

_____   f. Apply shellac, varnish, or lacquer.

8. Bleaching is one step in all standard finishes. (T or F)

9. The correct sandpaper to use between each coat of standard finish is
(one right)
a. 2.
b. 1/0.
c. 5/0.
d. 1.

_____   10. Sealing protects the topcoat from scratches and dents. (T or F)

_____   11. A wash coat consists of one part shellac and seven parts _____.

_____   12. Open-grained woods require a liquid filler. (T or F)

_____   13. Sealer should never be applied over filler. (T or F)

_____   14. Two or more topcoats are usually required for a good finish. (T or F)

BEGINNING WOODWORK STUDENT GUIDE

Chapter 39
Care of Finishing Supplies
(Text pages 207-209)

_____ 1. Most finishing supplies catch fire easily. (T or F)

_____ 2. It is a good idea to store cans of finishing material upside down. (T or F)

_____ 3. Always pour thinned finishes back into their original container. (T or F)

_____ 4. A shellac brush should be cleaned in alcohol. (T or F)

_____ 5. Enamel brushes are kept in a 50/50 mixture of varnish and _____.

Match the brush in the left-hand column with the solvent in which it should be stored in the right-hand column.

_____   6. shellac brush   a. half varnish and half turpentine
_____   7. paint and stain brush   b. alcohol
_____   8. varnish brush   c. one part turpentine and two parts linseed oil

Match the description in the left-hand column with the finishing material in the right-hand column.

_____   9. turpentine   a. yellowish oil from flaxseed
_____   10. alcohol   b. wood drippings or chemicals
_____   11. linseed oil   c. resin drippings of pine trees
_____   12. benzine   d. white powder from lava
_____   13. rottenstone   e. petroleum or paraffin oil
_____   14. rubbing oil   f. reddish-brown or greyish-black substance for smooth-
_____   15. pumice   ing and rubbing
_____   16. steel wool   g. colorless liquid made from petroleum
                                    h. steel shavings

_____ 17. Wet-dry abrasive paper may be used with water for sanding between finish coats. (T or F)

Chapters 40 and 41
Staining Wood and Applying Fillers
(Text pages 209-213)

_____ 1. The most common kinds of stains are oil, water, and _____.

_____ 2. Oil stain can be made by mixing ground-in-oil pigment with turpentine. (T or F)

_____ 3. Oil stain is the cheapest kind of stain. (T or F)

_____ 4. Water stain is usually mixed with one ounce of powder to a _____ of water.

_____ 5. It is better to apply one heavy coat of stain than to put on two lighter coats. (T or F)

_____ 6. Before applying oil stain to end grain, apply a thin coat of _____ _____.

_____ 7. Dip the brush about _____ of the way into the oil stain.

Match the woods on the left with the kinds of filler they require. Answers may be used more than once.

_____ 8. maple

_____ 9. mahogany

_____ 10. poplar

_____ 11. walnut

_____ 12. oak

_____ 13. cherry

_____ 14. hickory

a. paste filler
b. liquid filler
c. no filler

_____ 15. A liquid filler can be made by thinning paste filler with (one right)
a. linseed oil.
b. turpentine.
c. shellac.
d. varnish.

_____ 16. When applying a paste filler, brush both with and across the grain. (T or F)

Date _____   Name _____

Score (27 possible) _____

Chapters 42, 43, 44, and 45

Applying Finishes

(Text pages 214-221)

_____   1. When a shellac topcoat will be applied, a _____ stain should be used.

_____   2. Shellac can be used on projects that will get damp. (T or F)

_____   3. Shellac is available in two colors, _____ and white.

_____   4. Standard shellac is called four-pound cut, which means that there are four pounds of shellac mixed with a _____ of alcohol.

_____   5. For a wash coat, use one part shellac to _____ parts alcohol.

_____   6. For a first coat the shellac should be mixed one part shellac to _____ part alcohol.

_____   7. When applying shellac, dip the brush about _____ of the way into the shellac.

_____   8. When applying shellac, always go over the same area at least twice. (T or F)

_____   9. To apply shellac, begin at the edges. (T or F)

_____   10. For the second coat mix one part shellac to _____ part(s) alcohol.

_____   11. Shellac dries quickly. (T or F)

_____   12. The correct kind of varnish to use on surfaces that may become damp is _____ varnish.

_____   13. A clean cloth dampened with turpentine to which two or three tablespoons of varnish have been added is called a _____ rag.

_____   14. Varnish should be diluted for the first coat. (T or F)

_____   15. Varnish should be leveled out with the tip of the brush. (T or F)

_____   16. To apply varnish, begin at the edges and work toward the center. (T or F)

_____   17. All lacquers are clear. (T or F)

_____   18. When applying a lacquer finish, use alcohol for thinning the materials and cleaning the brushes. (T or F)

_____   19. Several light coats of lacquer should be sprayed on a surface rather than one heavy one. (T or F)

_____   20. A surface should be sanded between coats of lacquer. (T or F)

_____   21. A finish that soaks into the wood is called a _____ or wipe-on finish.

_____   22. When using a finish that soaks into the wood, only the first coat needs to be sanded. (T or F)

(Continued on next page)

_____

_____

_____

_____

_____

23. Sealacell is a moisture-repellent, penetrating wood sealer that is applied over _____ wood.

24. Varno wax is a blend of _____ and waxes.

25. A Minwax finish need not be rubbed after each coat. (T or F)

26. To produce a Danish oil finish, penetrating _____ is needed.

27. Danish oil finishes must be reapplied once a year. (T or F)

BEGINNING WOODWORK STUDENT GUIDE

Chapter 46
Applying Paint and Enamel
(Text pages 222-223)

_____   1. Paints and enamels are transparent. (T or F)

_____   2. For a hard, glossy surface, use enamel. (T or F)

_____   3. The coloring matter in paint is called _____.

_____   4. The liquid portion of paint is the _____.

_____   5. Latex paints have a(n) _____ base.

_____   6. Enamel paints usually have a(n) _____ base.

_____   7. To apply paint to small areas, use a 2- or 3-inch brush. (T or F)

_____   8. Before applying enamel, cover knots and sap streaks with a wash coat of _____.

_____   9. When painting, the primer coat will completely hide the wood surface. (T or F)

10. Arrange in numerical order these steps for applying paint. Each answer is worth one point.

_____   a. Thin the primer, if necessary.

_____   b. Allow to dry; sand lightly with 6/0 sandpaper.

_____   c. Apply paint just as it comes from the can.

_____   d. Fill holes; seal knots.

_____   e. Apply the undercoat.

Date _____   Name _____

Score (14 possible) _____

Chapter 47
Decorating the Surface of Wood
(Text pages 223-226)

_____

_____

_____

_____

_____

_____

1. Basswood and poplar are good woods to use for woodburning. (T or F)

2. Most burning tools come with several _____ so that the design can be varied.

3. Use a _____ to guide the tool when you make straight lines.

4. To prevent stains from bleeding after woodburning, apply a thin coat of _____ to the area you don't want darkened.

5. When applying a decal to a wood surface, always apply a thin coat of _____ first.

6. After a decal has been applied to a wood surface, cover it with a coat of shellac or wax. (T or F)

7. Arrange in numerical order these steps in using color pencils on wood. Each answer is worth one point.

_____

_____

_____

_____

_____

_____

_____

   a. Transfer the design to the wood.

   b. Apply varnish. When dry, buff with steel wool.

   c. Buff; apply a coat of wax.

   d. Sand the wood with 3/0 sandpaper; wipe clean.

   e. Apply a coat of varnish.

   f. Color the design.

8. For metal tooling, use a small wooden _____ to press the shape into the metal.

9. The metal used for tooling is usually _____.

Chapter 48
Drill Press, Scroll Saw, and Band Saw
(Text pages 227-236)

_____

_____

_____

_____

_____

_____

a. _____

b. _____

c. _____

d. _____

e. _____

f. _____

g. _____

_____

_____

_____

_____

_____

_____

_____

_____

1. Machine auger bits have a straight _____ and a brad point.

2. Hand auger bits can be used in the drill press. (T or F)

3. A 15-inch drill press measures _____ inches from the center of the chuck to the column.

4. Fast speeds on the drill press should be used for large diameter cutting tools and hardwoods. (T or F)

5. For drilling small holes on the drill press, use a _____ drill.

6. The scroll saw is used to cut inside and outside _____.

7. Name the parts of the scroll saw shown in Fig. 48-A.

48-A

8. Figure 48-A shows a rocker-action scroll saw. (T or F)

9. A 15-inch scroll saw will cut to the center of a _____ inch circle.

10. A scroll saw blade should be selected so that at least _____ teeth touch the work at all times.

11. The blade should be installed in the scroll saw with the teeth pointing _____.

12. Number in correct order the steps in cutting on a scroll saw.

    a. Start in the waste stock.

    b. Stand in front of the scroll saw.

    c. Apply forward pressure with your thumbs.

    d. Carefully guide the work so that the saw stays outside the layout line.

    e. Turn the work slowly at sharp corners.

13. The blade guide on a band saw should be moved close to the work to be done. (T or F)

14. To get a good, clean cut, work should be fed through the band saw quickly. (T or F)

Date _____   Name _____

Score (17 possible) _____

Chapter 49
Other Machine (Power) Tools
(Text pages 236-249)

_____ 1. Operating power tools requires less skill than using hand tools. (T or F)

_____ 2. To change the depth of cut on a jointer, the front _____ is adjusted up or down.

_____ 3. When wood is surfaced on a jointer, it is held against the table and the _____.

_____ 4. Planing should be done with the grain. (T or F)

_____ 5. Protect your hands from the jointer head by always using a _____ _____.

_____ 6. When lumber comes from the mill in rough thickness, the _____ is used to surface it.

_____ 7. Such operations as crosscutting and ripping can be done well on the circular saw. (T or F)

_____ 8. A circular saw blade that can be used both for crosscutting and ripping is called a _____ blade.

_____ 9. A circular saw _____ is needed for all types of ripping operations.

_____ 10. When ripping on the circular saw, stand directly back of the stock. (T or F)

_____ 11. When ripping narrow stock on the circular saw, a _____ _____ should be used to push the stock past the blade.

_____ 12. Scrap stock should never be removed from the circular saw with the fingers. (T or F)

_____ 13. The radial-arm saw will perform the same operations as the circular saw. (T or F)

_____ 14. More wood lathes are used by the home craftsperson than in industry. (T or F)

_____ 15. For sanding operations, the most popular machine is the combination belt and _____ sander.

_____ 16. Disk sanding should be done on the half of the disk revolving upward. (T or F)

_____ 17. The belt sander is used mainly for _____ sanding.

44

BEGINNING WOODWORK STUDENT GUIDE
Protected by Copyright

Date _____ Name _____

Score (17 possible) _____

Chapter 50
Portable Power Tools
(Text pages 251-261)

a. _____

b. _____

c. _____

1. Name the three most often used portable power tools.

2. Two safety systems designed in tools to protect you from electrical shock are:

   a. _____ grounding and

   b. _____ insulation.

3. A _____ drill is more suitable for drilling at slow speeds.

4. To adjust the depth of cut of a router, raise or lower the router _____.

_____

_____

_____

_____

5. The width of a router cut is determined by the _____.

6. Shaping an edge with a router requires the use of a bit with a _____.

_____

_____

7. When using a portable belt sander, the sander should be lowered so that the heel touches the work first. (T or F)

8. Sanding is actually done on a portable belt sander on the _____ stroke.

_____

9. _____ sanding is sometimes done first to obtain a level surface.

_____

10. A saber saw can make long cuts as accurately and quickly as a circular saw. (T or F)

_____

11. The base or skid of a saber saw should extend _____ inch in front of the blade.

12. Blades are installed in the saber saw with the teeth pointing _____.

_____

13. The angle adjustment on a portable circular saw tilts the base as much as _____ degrees.

_____

14. The good side of stock should be facing _____ when cutting with a portable circular saw.

Chapters 51 and 52
Lumbering and Forest Products
(Text pages 262-270)

_____

1. Privately owned forest lands supply about 60 percent of the nation's lumber. (T or F)

_____

2. About 28 percent of the lumber is obtained from public lands, mostly in national forests. (T or F)

_____

3. The earliest method of transporting logs to mills was in rivers and streams. (T or F)

_____

4. Most logs today are transported to the mills in _____, boats, or railroad cars.

_____

5. When logs first arrive at the mill, they are _____ to estimate the amount of lumber each log will produce.

_____

6. Logs are cut into lumber by huge band saws. (T or F)

_____

7. The uses for wood and wood products number about (one right)
   a. 25.
   b. 10,000.
   c. 1,500.
   d. 100.

_____

8. The most common way of cutting softwood veneer is by the _____ cut method.

_____

9. Plywood made with five layers is more likely to warp than plywood made with three layers. (T or F)

_____

10. The standard plywood sheet is _____ feet by 8 feet.

_____

11. The percentage of lumber used to make pulp for paper is about (one right)
    a. 20 percent.
    b. 30 percent.
    c. 50 percent.
    d. 60 percent.

_____

12. Trees add to the _____ supply.

_____

13. Plastics can be made from wood products. (T or F)

_____

14. Branches, bark, and sawdust are waste products thrown away by lumber mills. (T or F)

Date _____ Name _____

Score (16 possible) _____

Chapters 53 and 54
Manufacturing and Construction
(Text pages 271-296)

_____   1. Money used to buy what a company needs is called _____.

_____   2. New knowledge and materials are found through the efforts of _____.

_____   3. The _____ department sets up standards for testing new materials, processes, and techniques.

_____   4. Products made by mass production methods are (one right)
      a. perfect.
      b. identical.
      c. different.
      d. expensive.

_____   5. In planning to mass-produce a product, _____ research should be done to find out the kinds of products that will sell best.

_____   6. To discover construction problems, a _____ should be built.

_____   7. A device fastened to a machine for holding pieces in the right position for cutting or shaping is called a _____.

_____   8. A device that guides the cutting tool and holds the product or part is called a _____.

_____   9. _____ plans show what a house will look like from the front, the back, and the sides.

_____   10. A written list of all materials needed to build a house is called the _____.

_____   11. The bottom part of the foundation wall that supports the weight of the house is called the _____.

_____   12. The framework for the walls of a house is made of pieces of wood called _____.

_____   13. Ready-made joist-and-rafter units that look like triangles with braces are called prefabricated _____.

_____   14. The most popular wall in modern home interiors is the plastered wall. (T or F)

_____   15. The worker on the building team who installs the interior trim is the _____.

_____   16. The worker responsible for the walks and other poured concrete units such as steps and patios is the _____.

Date _____   Name _____

Score (14 possible) _____

_____ 1. The number of people who work directly or indirectly in occupations related to forests and the use of lumber is over (*one right*)
   a. half a million.
   b. one million.
   c. two million.
   d. five million.

_____ 2. The largest group of skilled craft workers in the United States are _____.

_____ 3. The young person who works with an experienced carpenter learning the skills of the trade is called (*one right*)
   a. a helper.
   b. a student.
   c. an apprentice.
   d. a junior carpenter.

_____ 4. A person who makes the shapes from which metal castings are poured in the foundry is called a _____.

_____ 5. Most workers in the furniture industry are highly skilled. (T or F)

_____ 6. The two major parts of a computer system are the hardware and the _____.

_____ 7. The letters used to describe the "brain" or central processing unit of a computer are _____.

_____ 8. The term computer-aided design means that a product has a built-in computer. (T or F)

_____ 9. These devices can be used to change a design on a monitor screen: (*one wrong*)
   a. mouse.
   b. cat.
   c. light pen.
   d. digitizer.

_____ 10. An automatic machine controlled by a computer is called a _____.

_____ 11. A laser is a device that amplifies, strengthens, and concentrates light. (T or F)

_____ 12. An electronic tool for surveying is called a laser _____.

_____ 13. Electronically controlled power tools contain a _____.

_____ 14. Airless spraying does not produce the _____ associated with air spraying.